ON THE WAY TO THE ISLAND

ON THE WAY

Middletown, Connecticut

TO THE ISLAND

BY DAVID FERRY

WESLEYAN UNIVERSITY PRESS

11/1962
am. Lit.

Copyright © 1953, 1954, 1955, 1956, 1957, 1959, 1960 by David Ferry

Some of these poems have appeared previously. I am indebted to the editors of the following publications in which poems have been published: *Best Poems of 1955*, "Lines for a Dead Poet"; *Harvard Advocate*, "The Late-Hour Poem"; *i.e. The Cambridge Review*, "Johnson on Pope"; *Kenyon Review*, "The Embarkation for Cythera," "The Sage by the Seashore," "My Parents en Route"—also "The Bird," "The Milkmaid," "The Soldier," there published under the joint title "Three Poems About Vanity"; *The Nation*, "Out in the Cold"; *New Poems by American Poets No. 2*, "On the Way to the Island," "The Unawkward Singers," "Poem About Waking," "The Antagonist," "Out of That Sea"; *Paris Review*, "Elegiac," "The Good Man," "Learning from History"; *Partisan Review*, "In the Dark." The third, fourth, fifth, sixth, and seventh stanzas of "Adam's Dream" appeared originally in *The New Yorker*.

I am also very grateful to Elizabeth Ames and to the Trustees of Yaddo, Saratoga Springs, N. Y., for their hospitality during the summer of 1957.

Library of Congress catalog card number: 60–13156
Manufactured in the United States of America
First edition

FOR A. D. F.

CONTENTS

The Embarkation for Cythera   13

Adam's Dream   14

To the Fabulous Constellation   16

Elegiac   17

On the Way to the Island   18

From the Dream Country   19

The Sage by the Seashore   20

Johnson on Pope   21

My Parents en Route   22

Lines for a Dead Poet   23

What It Does   24

The Late-Hour Poem   25

Poem About Waking   26

The Good Man   27

Learning from History   28

The Antagonist   30

The Unawkward Singers   31

Out of That Sea   32

The Bird   33

The Milkmaid   34

The Soldier   35

Dog and Fox   36

Out in the Cold   37

In the Dark   38

For the Birthday of Miss Marianne Moore,
    Whenever Her Birthday Is   39

At a Low Bar   40

A Farewell   42

Musings of Mind and Body   43

Descriptive   44

The Beach at Evening   45

Sonnet de Ronsard   46

Sonnet of Ronsard   47

The Crippled Girl, the Rose   48

Poem   49

Aubade   50

ON THE WAY TO THE ISLAND

THE EMBARKATION FOR CYTHERA

—after Watteau

The picnic-goers beautified themselves,
And then set sail for Cythera, with jugs
To keep their coffee hot, martinis cold,
And hampers full of music. The water shone
For them that day, and like a street of jewels
Lay between their land and the island.

Their cockle hull was pretty, white and gold
As the Mozarteum, and their laughter picked
Its way, nicely as tunes of proper jump,
From port to starboard, gentlemen to ladies,
And return. They played their cards right, whiling
The day away by smiling and by thinking

Of the times to come, the banquets in the grove
On the antless island of that ancient idol
Love, the girl who rose to be the pearl
To deck them out. Thinking of her, each lady
Fingered her necklace, and sweet music tattled
From the spinet of her desire; each lord

Touched at his sleeve for the ace he'd hidden there.

ADAM'S DREAM

The sycamores and sidewalks of
His neighborhood were private park
And dark retreat, where he could walk
In congress sweet

With his kind neighbors, sleep and love,
And where their gossip, or nice talk,
Discriminated beast from bird
By proper word:

Adam yawned, and there were cats;
Blinked, and there were antelopes;
Stretched, and everywhere he reached
A mile of meadow bloomed.

He cocked his eye, and fishes leaped
In every brook to praise him;
He rose to walk, and rabbits ran
As couriers to every green
Community to tell of him.

He only glanced at any tree,
Its birds at once began to sing;
He nodded, and the region budded;
He put the bloom on everything.

He was the lord of all the park,
And he was lonely in the dark,
Till Eve came smiling out of his side
To be his bride.

"Sweet rib," he said, astonished at her,
"This is *my* green environ!"
Eve answered no word, but for reply
The wilderness was in her eye.

Adam awoke, the snow had come,
And drifts of daylight covered the park;
And his sweet friends, and their sweet talk,
Were dumb.

TO THE FABULOUS CONSTELLATION

Beautiful alien light, the lovers lie
In trouble in the park, whose summer leaves obstruct
Their sight of what's been shaped for them in stars;
Or, when the cold fall draws those leaves to earth,
Their icy eyes and smoky breaths construct
Other configurations in the sky.

Where you are formed in foreign splendor is
Nor heat nor cold, nor none of the changes lovers know:
Plato either made you or some other
Imagination of no weather shaped
Beyond our scope, beyond our leaves and snow,
To show how obstinate lovers ought to be wise.

The lovers lie in trouble in the park.
The cold fall draws the leaves to earth around them.
Good angels of these lovers, come, surround them,
Be as if summer foliage in the dark

Gathered about them, guarding them from all harms.
Hot ignorant lovers, they don't know how they are taken
Far from the summer sun, out of their season.
Each burns in the brightness there of the other's arms.

Thinking of them, I think of my own death coming,
When I shall seasonless lie in the unloving earth,
And of the deaths of all others, as of the death
Of these lovers, locked in the ice, and burning.

Persisting in bliss, all lovers are coming to ill,
And by their heat have caught this mortal chill.

ON THE WAY TO THE ISLAND

After we fled away from the shuddering dock,
The sea upheld us, would not let us go
Nor drown us, and we danced all night in the dark,
Till we woke to discover the deck was made of glass,
All glass, and, leaning together, we lovers looked down,
Say a hundred miles, say a million years, and there
Were the fish, huge, munching, graceless, flashing
Their innocent frightening scales in the dark!

My lady wears brilliants in her hair, and the sun
Makes their fakery sparkle, so beautiful
Is she my lady, so pitiful is she,
Her white arms so naked after those scales,
Her coquetry pretty after those monsters
Beginning her history there in the deep dark.
My lady, I love you because of the dark,
Over which your glass slippers so ignorantly danced!

FROM THE DREAM COUNTRY

There, by those streams, where every fish
Rose to the bait of every wish,
We walked. The small deer by our side
Trembled at terrors they descried,
And each, within its tawny eye,
Kept secrets of something there that we,
Mistaking in our ignorance,
Took to be changeless innocence.
And so, as in every field we walked,
The grasses of our pleasures talked.

But there, in the wood, the oriole hid
Within its splendid breast a tide
So terrible as to wash us free
Of that dream's bank, on which to be
Was to be deaf to the terror sung
In the dream country's charmèd tongue.
That tongue its knowledge could not declare.
Nevertheless, in that sweet air
Implicit it was, and in the color
Of lion's back, and bee-hung flower.

So it is that now we range
In sober love, in chance and change.

THE SAGE BY THE SEASHORE

Now the tree
That had been stone
Is stone again:
Another age
With notice none
Of what had gone
And come again
Of mirth and pride
Is finally done.

Now the one
And only sage
Faces the sea,
And every tide
Registers on
His roaring page
The change of bone
To ice, and stone
To flower and sea.

JOHNSON ON POPE

—from *The Lives of the Poets*

He was protuberant behind, before;
Born beautiful, he had grown up a spider;
Stature so low, he could not sit at table
Like taller men; in middle life so feeble
He could not dress himself, nor stand upright
Without a canvas bodice; in the long night
Made servants peevish with his demands for coffee;
Trying to make his spider's legs less skinny,
He wore three pair of stockings, which a maid
Had to draw on and off; one side was contracted.
But his face was not displeasing, his eyes were vivid.

He found it very difficult to be clean
Of unappeasable malignity;
But in his eyes the shapeless vicious scene
Composed itself; of folly he made beauty.

Dead to the world in love my parents lie,
Snoring, and solemn as princes catafalqued,
Their dreaming toes turned upward to the sky.

Heavy with sleepy beauty, my mother walked
Last night, in her dream, in a world unknown
To me, to her, or to my father; she talked,
In that landscape, though mutely as a stone,
In colloquy with princesses of state
More marvelous than any that has been,
Waking. This of her dream I would relate.

My father, brave without fierceness, I have seen,
As after the golden tawny-yellow beast he went,
The mightiest hunter, emblazoned with exploits brave,
No fear in his look, but pity, and brave content;
My father was sent to chase that beast and have
The colloquy stately and endless argument
Of the hunt. Thus through his dream did he move.

I think, of their bedclothes' tangle and humble sleep
I make up a legend, though false as their dream
Yet true as their bodies' submissions. The steep
Sea shudders and wallows as, snoring, they steam,
Laborious ships that I love, to the deep
Tideless center and pitch of my filial dream.

LINES FOR A DEAD POET

Here lies the poet, deaf and dumb.
Into his ear no sound can come,

Into his eye no sight
Of life, or limb, or the marvelous light.

Ice are his eyes, that once were seas,
In which dwelt creatures more than these

He left us by his going there,
Into the earth, out of the air

Where verity did once reside,
Of the ear the grace, of the eye the pride.

The tongue lies useless now that was
The maker of such strange, sweet laws

We were his citizens, and stayed
In a country that his poems made.

WHAT IT DOES

The sea bit,
As they said it would,
And the hill slid,
As they said it would,
And the poor dead
Nodded agog
The poor head.

O topmost lofty
Tower of Troy,
The poem apparently
Speaks with joy
Of terrible things.
Where is the pleasure
The poetry brings?

Tell if you can,
What does it make?
A city of man
That will not shake,
Or if it shake,
Shake with the splendor
Of the poem's pleasure.

In an hour of furious clarity,
By liquor made,
Full of a fierce charity,
My harp I played.
I made a loud uproar!
I went in turn
From door to every door.
Marry or burn!
Love your neighbor, I cried.
Pity the poor
Divided people, who side
By side here lie,
Transfixed in sleep; and shadow
Covers each eye.
On house and house the echo
Rang and rebounded.
My harp made everybody know
How brave I sounded!

POEM ABOUT WAKING

I knew once
In your embrace
The need that thence
I soon must pass
And find my age
Some other place,
And thus in rage
I loved, alas!

The good man went his way in personal freedom;
His body shone as if by its own consent;
He had no king, and was himself his kingdom;
He was both just and kind in government.

His gesture made of air a form and figure;
His voice made leaves speak stanzas in his praise;
He praised the leaves, and everything in nature;
Majestic was his mien, charming his ways.

When he laughed aloud, the mountains held their sides;
When he wept soft the wind hung on the meadow;
Obedient was the moon, careful the tides;
There was no danger, not in any shadow.

There was no good man, though we thought of him;
Yet everything came true because of him.

They said, my saints, my slogan-sayers sang,
Be good, my child, in spite of all alarm.
They stood, my fathers, tall in a row and said,
Be good, be brave, you shall not come to harm.
I heard them in my sleep and muttering dream,
And murmuring cried, How shall I wake to this?
They said, my poets, singers of my song,
We cannot tell, since all we tell you is
But history, we speak but of the dead.
And of the dead they said such history
(Their beards were blazing with the truth of it)
As made of much of me a mystery.

As in my covered sleep I dreamed of waking,
I dreamed that I went solitary roving
Over the sunk cities of my ancestors,
Over a darkness, over a deepness swimming.
Dreaming of this I was when they spoke to me.
Lovers they bragged of, long since dead and gone,
Whose ashes through the ages of their deaths
Patiently break. Long since are they gone.
What could these lovers tell me in my sleep?
Donne's lovers saw another hemisphere,
Completing for each the world, as eye to eye
They pressed, than what I see. I am, they were.

They said, my sages, my truth-tellers told
Tall tales of captains gone into their graves.
How pitiful they fell that had been bold!
The little that *they* tell is, history saves
Little, and what it saves is hardly told,
And what is hardly told is hardly heard.

Something repeats, they say. Of what it is,
Or how be told, these captains have no word,
Soldiers, who pressed a distant battleground
With a proud foot made proud by still another
Image of what we were. Now they are sunk
Under the wave of earth. I am, they were.

I dreamed all this as in my childhood I
Lay patiently covered up, waiting for morning.
Lovers there were, and captains, crowding my room,
Sages, and poets, telling me almost nothing
But brave, be brave, we tell as to a child
What can be told only in his awakening.
Loudly my lordly moralizers spoke,
Calling me from my sleep, though still in my dreaming.

THE ANTAGONIST

I saw a man come down to the furious sea.
He had a beard, and in that beard were birds.
He stood between the sea and a green tree
And brushed those birds away. They flew like words
Out of his crystal beard, they flew away,
Skittering into the sky, and soon were gone.
This was a man who had a crystal eye,
And all turned crystal that he looked upon.
Divinity flowers here, he said, and here
Also. And in the wind. How crystal-clear
Divinity blooms, in sea, and wind, and wood!
It is like light, and light like God, and good!

Then sure enough the world was all one flower
Of crystal light, and lost in the light was I,
Was the tree, were the birds, and the fish in his power
Were lost in the light-lost sea, till stubbornly I
Stood still in that light and tore and tore with my tongue
At that prisoning flower, imagining till all the birds
Sang loud again in that wood, till loud the fish sang
In the furious sea, echoing my fierce words,
Fantastic birds roaring in *that* green wood!
I *would not* give assent to what he said!
I stood in that place till crystal lay all about me!
Imagine your heaven, I cried, but do it without me!

Self-praise is a wonderful thing!
It causes all the birds to sing:
The sparrow's brag, thrush's conceit,
They make the whole world cheerly repeat,
Cheerly repeat their praise!

For any lark there is no other,
No father, mother, sister, brother,
No sweet wife, nor no dear love;
The dove's the pool in which the dove,
Loving, admires his ways.

Wind out of the swan's throat
His final, operatic note:
Impassioned on himself he dies,
Knowing the world is him, is his
By his self-celebration.

Master man cannot so please
Himself with the confidence of these.
Thus, clumsily his song is sung,
Thick praise by a thick tongue
For its own limitation.

OUT OF THAT SEA

As shepherd and shepherdess, how many summers had we
Sung mourning and praising? Our sheep were lulling and
        drowsing;
Like bottomless pools our cattle lay lolling long.
Love, said our pipes, love, love, cried the cattle bird skimming
The piebald depths of those cows. All afternoon drifted;
And dreaming we lay as the light and the sea shade shifted.

It was then that we drowned in the sleep and deep dream of
        that beauty,
Thanking our deaths as we turned, slowly and slowly,
Falling through light we fell to the golden floor.
We alighted like angels, and all in our dreaming we danced,
Fantastic, slow, wonderful turning and courtesy!
The sea caves rang with the wonder, fish sang for the beauty!

Then together we rose, and together, and hand in hand,
We went through a landscape neither ideal nor pretty,
Coming to ruin. Nearby, in a hickory tree,
The wise old owl sat mute. From his eye a glare
Shone loud and clear in the calm evening air.
From the hoot of that eye we shrank in our sudden fear,

And together, I turning to you, you turning to me,
We saw how our hands came wrinkled out of that sea.

Carefully, and as if fearfully,
And minding of itself in its own fine feather,
Though modestly, and mildly in its finding,
This bird, submissive to the weather,
Storm, wind, the birds' peril,
This bird I saw that could not see
Me in my loud body standing;
Watchful the bird was only of itself,
With softliest mutter and flatter of itself.
Brave bird, be heedful of yourself
In the good weather!

A practised gesture of her practised hand,
So ivory, and so bejeweled with finger tip,
Made all our party put on her livery,
Seeking to pay her lip service, singing her
Songs she had no mind to hear from us.

All brilliant baldheads in our row gave back
Her radiance, so that her motions were our wit,
Reflections of the notions in our skulls,
Which beat with poems to her practised skills.
We made a lady of her in our poems.

She was a milkmaid once, whose head we'd turned,
That, turning, in the mirror saw itself
Under its truest guise, faithfullest aspect.
We brought her to the city in our songs,
Mistress most wise of the city we brought her to.

Alone, released from us, her mirror told
The same tale twice, the lesson she'd learned well.
She glittered in her eye, her buttery skin
Turned satin, silk, or damask, ivory, pearl,
All that we'd sung of her in our amorous songs.

O brave milkmaid, we cried, as she stepped out,
Dressed in her borrowed finery, flouting us,
The nose turned high that country suns had peeled,
O brave milkmaid, be brave when finery tatters!
You are not wise as us in these city matters!

Saturday afternoon. The barracks is almost empty.
The soldiers are almost all on overnight pass.
There is only me, writing this letter to you,
And one other soldier, down at the end of the room,
And a spider, that hangs by the thread of his guts,
His tenacious and delicate guts, Swift's spider,
All self-regard, or else all privacy.
The dust drifts in the sunlight around him, as currents
Lie in lazy drifting schools in the vast sea.
In his little sea the spider lowers himself
Out of his depth. He is his own diving bell,
Though he cannot see well. He observes no fish,
And sees no wonderful things. His unseeing guts
Are his only hold on the world outside himself.
I love you, and miss you, and I find you hard to imagine.
Down at the end of the room, the other soldier
Is getting ready, I guess, to go out on pass.
He is shining his boots. He sits on the edge of his bunk,
Private, submissive, and heedful of himself,
And, bending over himself, he is his own nest.
The slightest sound he makes is of his being.
He is his mother, and nest, wife, brother, and father.
His boots are bright already, yet still he rubs
And rubs till, brighter still, they are his mirror.
And in this mirror he observes, I guess,
His own submissiveness. He is far from home.

DOG AND FOX

The quick brown fox jumps over the lazy dog.
He does indeed, and the dog, who does not doze,
Jumps after the fox and catches him in his jaws.
Pray, citizen Smart, can you tell me please what cause
For enmity between such pleasant creatures?
I have looked everywhere for learnèd teachers
To latin me this: why does the lazy dog
Not *waltz* with the quick brown fox, and they together,
As true friends should, brave fair and stormy weather?

The sun shines in the ice of my country
As my smile glitters in the mirror of my devotion.
Flat is the scene there. There are a few scrub bushes.
I live on the edge of the land. The frozen sea
Lies locked for a thousand miles to the north, to the Pole.

Meagre my mouth, and my knuckles sharp and white.
They will hurt when I hit. I fish for a fish
So thin and sharp in the tooth as to suit my malice.
It stares like any fish, but it knows a lot,
Knows what I know. Astonishment it has not.

I have a hut to which I go at night.
Sometimes there is no night, and the midnight sun
And I sit up all night and fish for that fish.
We huddle over the ice, the two of us.

I wandered in my mind as in the dark.
I stumbled over a chair, ran into a wall,
Or another wall, I wandered down a hall,
And into another room, the same as before.
I stumbled against a wall, I felt the floor
Carefully with each foot, I found a door,
And into another room, the same as before.
I wandered in my mind, I was in the dark.
I sidled up against another wall,
I shouldered along it, searching for a door,
And found one, opening out into a hall
That led to another room, the same as before.
In fear I tuned my voice to a little tune,
A crazy tune that sang inside my head,
And followed the tune as one would follow a thread
That leads one to or from a minotaur.
And that tune led me back or forward mazily,
That sang inside my head so crazily!

I followed or fled at last into a hall
That had a little light. Down at the end
Of the hall, a long way off, two windows were,
And into the windows came a little light.
I followed down the hall as to a friend
Long since offended. Timidly I wore
An anxious smile, eager to please. The light
Grew brighter still, till at last to the end
Of the hall I came. What a wonderful sight!
I found that I was looking through my eyes!
Outside of myself what a beautiful landscape lies!

FOR THE BIRTHDAY OF MISS MARIANNE MOORE, WHENEVER HER BIRTHDAY IS

I

Let her look at a stone:
The stone becomes an apple,
The apple of her eye.
Nor is it only the stone:
Her eye becomes a hand
To hold the apple up,
Gently for the mind,
Which is the truest eye,
Kindly to look upon.

II

To squeeze from a stone its juice,
And find how sweet it is,
Is her art's happiness.

AT A LOW BAR

While in a bar I bore
Indignity with those
Others whose hearts were sore
Or sour or sick or such
As made them humankind,
I looked into my glass
To see if I could find
Something to give me ease.

Narcissus at the pool,
I looked lovingly at
My own disordered fool,
Who would not tell me much,
But stared patiently back.
He would not tell me what
I'd ever have or lack.
He would not tell me that.

I looked along the bar
And saw my fellow creature
Bravely standing there.
By word, sign, or touch,
I cried in my mute heart,
Tell me, be my teacher,
Be learnèd in that art,
What is my name and nature?

My pulse ticked in my wrist;
The noon hung around unawares;
Outside the traffic passed.
Like quiet cattle or such,

Standing about a pool,
Dumb, ignorant creatures,
My fellow, my self, my fool,
Ignorant of our natures.

A FAREWELL

Let the day fall like light out of the eye.
Out of the ear let its music go. From the touch
Let the touching of air retire. Remain in the dark,
Dumbly remain in the dark. What will they know
Of you then, or want, when, then, in the dark you remain?

Knowledge began with the pressure of light on the eye,
And the ear spun out of thin air its airy tune.
Let no vein flutter or flicker to signal the blood's
All but imperceptible errand. Does the skin
Shudder or shiver at all at least conjunction?

Shrink, then, into your dark, be locked up in yourself,
Shadow of shadow be in your nothing dark,
Oh be keep to yourself, be close, be moat, be wall
All dark. Hush. Hear hush. Vanish. Know nothing.
How then will the daylight knock at the lid in vain!

MUSINGS OF MIND AND BODY

the mind

I am that thing the sea cast up, a shell
Within whose murmuring round the tide or wind
Murmur their old music. My coil is cunning,
Envy, malice, pity, contemplation . . .
The wave that cast me out upon this beach
An hour ago, where I sit singing alone,
Will lace me round with her green arms, come tide,
Come evening, and I will be gone.
Meanwhile, I hum to myself myself in a humming dream.

the body

I am that sea. What I cast up is mine,
Whether I choose to take it back or not.
The driest bloom that spreads its papery petal
Far inland bears my legend on its flowering.
Read my sign in the lizard's grin. My voice
Cries out in the falling flesh of the great Bathsheba.
The little dog that leaps up in the field
Leaps up as if to leap out of my reach.
But I will wash him down. And thou, my mind.

DESCRIPTIVE

Alone, I looked down through the afternoon:
A long lawn, a great tree, a field, and a fountain.
The whole day was full of its colors that moved
About, above, within, and of each other,
Like bodies in the blindnesses of love.
The whole day was alive with its own creating.
Nothing was still, would stay, and for awhile
I looked at all this as if it were all I wanted,
Colors and shapes, fluid as one another,
So that the tree, which seemed one moment a tree,
Seemed at another an inexhaustible fountain
Cascading about itself in a green fall
Of water that never fell, and the green lawn
Was the water that never fell, running away.

THE BEACH AT EVENING

The beach at this evening full
Tide is a fisherman's back,
Whose bright muscles of rock
Glisten and strain as they pull
The cast net of the sea
In with a full catch
Of pebble, shell, and other
Things that belong to the sea.

Quand vous serez bien vieille, au soir à la chandelle,
Assise auprès du feu, dévidant et filant,
Direz chantant mes vers, en vous émerveillant:
"Ronsard me célébrait du temps que j'étais belle."

Lors vous n'aurez servante oyant telle nouvelle,
Déjà sous le labeur à demi sommeillant,
Qui au bruit de mon nom ne s'aille réveillant,
Bénissant votre nom de louange immortelle.

Je serai sous la terre et, fantôme sans os,
Par les ombres myrteux je prendrai mon repos:
Vous serez au foyer une vieille accroupie,

Regrettant mon amour et votre fier dédain.
Vivez, si m'en croyez, n'attendez à demain:
Cueillez dès aujourd'hui les roses de la vie.

     —Pierre de Ronsard (1524–1585)

When you are very old, at night, by candlelight,
Sitting up close to the fire, unwinding or winding the thread,
Marveling you will murmur, telling over the songs of the dead,
"Ronsard praised this body before it became this fright."

Not one of your companions, dozing over her spinning,
But, hearing you say these things in her old woman's dream,
Will be startled half-awake to bless your famous name
For the praise it had deserved of my immortal singing.

I will be under the earth, my body nothing at all,
Taking its rest at last, under the dark myrtle;
There you'll be by the fire, a hunched-up old woman

That held off my love for a long look in the mirror.
Listen to what I say, don't wait for tomorrow:
These flowers in their blossom go quickly out of season.

It was as if a flower bloomed as if
Its muttering root and stem had suddenly spoken,
Uttering on the air a poem of summer,
The rose the utterance of its root and stem.
Thus her beautiful face, the crippled girl's,
Was like the poem spoken by her body.

The richness of her face: most generous
In what it keeps; giving in its having.
The rose reserves the sweetness that it yields,
Petal on petal, telling its own silence,
Her beauty saying from its thorny stalk
That what it is is kept as it is given.

—to the Memory of G.E.F., Jr.

The ancient cup of tears, the pastoral legend,
Hid in the wood from which we've long since strayed,
Darkest of clearest pools, in whose reflection,
Or magnified or simplified, perfected,
The motions of our childhood lost were held
Or moving in the motion of the slight
Rippling as the light wind fled across it,
Is it the pool in which we cannot look now,
Nor drink from the dark freshness of that source
From which the pure words sprang that could be spoken
To utter a sorrow impersonal as legend?

AUBADE

If the early morning were like the dewy steaming
Rising of cloudy brightness
Out of the shadowy gardens of this sleep;
Were like this long last night's last dream, unquenched,
Drifting from the eye's
Opening splendor in the day's first instant;
Oh if the early morning
The slight smoke were of the banked fire of the sleeping
Ardor I watched so long,
So long heard breathe in the hearth of the heart's easy
Selfhood, knowing nothing but its sleeping:
Then were the morning one
Creature of your body's dear awakening.